INSECTS
WORLD OF
MINIATURE BEAUTY

With an introduction by Michael Tweedie

ORBIS BOOKS
LONDON

CONTENTS

All the photographs for this volume were specially taken by Carlo Bevilacqua; line illustrations are by Joyce Bee
Translated from the Italian of Umberto Parenti

© Orbis Publishing Limited, London 1971
© Istituto Geografico De Agostini, Novara 1968
Printed in Italy by IGDA, Novara
SBN 0 85613 101 6

**This book is to be returned on or before
the last date stamped below.**

In the modern world an increasingly large number of people dwell in cities and hardly come into contact with insects at all. To most of those living in less populated areas insects are at best a nuisance and at worst a pest, to be controlled or destroyed by the least expensive and most convenient means available.

Insects, however, are important. They are the most important of all the living creatures that share the lands of the world with us, with the exception of our domestic animals. On the one hand some of them threaten our health, or the food and other crops that we grow, so seriously that we are compelled to wage war on them, risking the hazards that war always brings to all the contestants, attacker and attacked alike. Some of the most serious problems of environmental pollution arise from the need to control carriers of disease and agricultural pests. On the other hand numerous insects are our allies in this very same warfare, since their prey is those insects whose numbers we are concerned to control. In some cases we actually enlist and promote the activities of these insect allies. An Australian species of ladybird beetle was imported into California to control the Cottony Cushion Scale insect which threatened to destroy the citrus fruit industry there. When the prickly pear cactus was introduced from subtropical America into Australia, it ran riot, covering millions of acres of valuable grazing and agricultural land. A small Argentinian moth, whose caterpillar will feed on prickly pear and nothing else, was brought to Australia and released. The moth throve and multiplied and the impenetrable cactus thickets melted away before the millions of tiny larvae that riddled and consumed them.

Many crops would be impossible to grow without the services of bees and flies that fertilize their seed by carrying pollen from flower to flower. Honeybees are now of more importance as pollinators of orchards than as producers of honey. Clover would not set seed at all in New Zealand until bumblebees were imported from Europe. Little solitary bees are now reared in millions in the United States to increase the seed yield of alfalfa.

Insects may be harmful or useful, but they are important to us in another entirely different way. Many of them are beautiful and a delight to watch in the wild and to examine as specimens with a lens or microscope. The loveliness of butterflies is very generally appreciated, but few people realise how intricately exquisite the jointed armour of a small beetle may be. This kind of beauty is revealed to perfection by skilled close-up photography of the kind displayed in the hundred-odd colour plates that illustrate this book. If its short text leads to your understanding insects rather better than before reading it, and the pictures help you to appreciate them, it will have fulfilled its purpose.

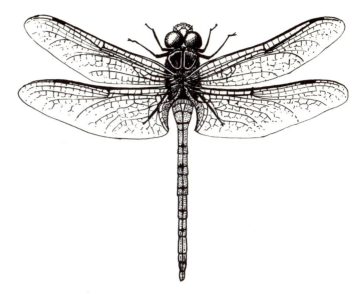

Insects learnt to fly before any other group of animals: fossil ancestors of the dragonfly (above) have been found dating from long before the dinosaurs.

The world of insects

In numbers of species, and probably of individuals as well, insects are the most numerous of all the animals that inhabit the land. Something rather less than a million different species have been described and named by entomologists, as students of insects are called, and at least twice as many more probably await discovery. It is sad to think that many of these will never be known to us because they will be exterminated by destruction of forest and other natural habitats before specimens of them are collected and examined. In an acre of grassland about 2½ million of the tiny insects called springtails are usually present, as well as many others such as beetles and various larvae. A similar area of tropical forest, from tree-tops to subsoil, probably harbours much larger populations of insects than this.

We have spoken of insects as animals; this is quite correct in the sense that they are members of the animal kingdom. At this point it will be well to see how they are related to other animals and how the insects themselves are classified.

There is a great division or phylum of the animal kingdom called the Arthropoda. It includes such creatures as prawns, crabs, sowbugs, spiders, scorpions, centipedes, millipedes – and insects. All these animals possess a hard jointed skeleton which encases the body and the limbs. The insects differ from the other arthropods mainly in two characteristics: when they are adult their bodies are divided in three distinct parts – head, thorax (or chest) and abdomen (or hind-body) – and they never have more than three pairs of legs. In addition most insects have one or two pairs of wings, which are possessed by none of the other arthropods. The legs and wings are always attached to the thorax. If you examine a fly or a bee you will find that it conforms closely to this typical insect pattern. A spider has four pairs of legs and its body is divided into only two parts; it is therefore not an insect.

In the complete system of classification of animals the insects form a class of the arthropod phylum and are divided in their turn into a number of orders. Mayflies form an order on their own, beetles another (though there are far more different kinds of beetles than of mayflies); the butterflies and moths make up a third. The following orders of insects are included among the colour plates in this book.

Ephemeroptera, Mayflies (plate 2). Delicate insects with (usually) two pairs of wings. Early stages always in water.

Odonata, Dragonflies and Damselflies (3, 4). Large predatory insects with two pairs of wings. Early stages in water.

Dictyoptera, Cockroaches and Mantises (5 to 9). Two groups that seem very distinct, but the structure of the wings and the mode of egg-laying indicate their affinity.

Phasmida, Stick-insects and Leaf-insects (10, 11). Large insects, mostly tropical, often showing remarkable camouflage.

Orthoptera, Grasshoppers, Locusts, Crickets (12 to 14). The hind legs are enlarged for jumping and the males often 'sing' by stridulation.

Dermaptera, Earwigs (15, 16). A small group, characterised by a pair of curved forceps at the hinder end.

Anopleura, Sucking lice (83). Small wingless insects, parasitic on mammals.

Hemiptera, Bugs (17 to 32). Mouthparts adapted for piercing and sucking, wings variously formed or absent, include bedbug, shieldbugs, aphids, cicadas.

Lepidoptera, Butterflies and Moths (34 to 49). Insects with two pairs of large wings covered with minute colored scales which often form beautiful patterns.

Diptera, Flies (50 to 56). Only one pair of wings, the hinder pair being transformed to form small balancing organs.

Coleoptera, Beetles (1, 33, 57 to 82, 84 to 94). The largest order of insects with about 275,000 known species. Usually two pairs of wings, the fore wings being transformed to horny sheaths which cover and protect the hind wings.

Hymenoptera, Wasps, Bees, Ants (95 to 110). Usually two pairs of wings, but worker ants are wingless. Often a venomous sting at the hind end of the body.

For many of the insects illustrated only Latin names are available. These may seem rather difficult and cumbersome, but the fact is that of the 900,000 or so

Typical members of three distinct orders of insect: Lepidoptera (above), Coleoptera (right) and Dermaptera (far right).

species that have received them only a minute fraction are known by names at all in the everyday speech of any country.

The chief advantage of the Latin names is that they are international. The butterfly shown on plate 47 is known to entomologists of every nation as *Nymphalis antiopa*. In North America it is called the Mourning Cloak, in Britain the Camberwell Beauty, in Germany Trauermantel (of which 'mourning cloak' is a translation), in France le Morio. Since it extends from Europe right across temperate Asia it must have received names in numerous other languages as well. Obviously the adoption of one name to be used everywhere by people who have a serious interest in insects must simplify the exchange of information between entomologists of various nationalities.

In this system each species or 'kind' of animal or plant is known by two names. The specific one (for example *antiopa*) identifies it precisely and the generic name defines its closest relationship with other species. Thus the Mourning Cloak *(Nymphalis antiopa)* is closely related to the European and Asian Large Tortoiseshell *(Nymphalis polychloros)*; the English names give no indication of this relationship. Latin names should always be printed in italics with only the generic name having an initial capital letter.

How insects grow

It was mentioned that insects, and other arthropods as well, have an external skeleton. This may seem a strange idea to us, but it is a fact that the jointed 'shell' of a crab's or beetle's leg plays the same part as the bones in that of a man. The muscles are attached to the different segments and by contracting cause them to pivot on their joints in order to make the movements necessary for walking. In the case of the man the muscles surround the bones of the leg, in that of the beetle they are contained in rigid tubes which play the same part as bones. Body movements are similarly controlled by muscles attached to the inside of its articulated shell.

The external skeleton also, of course, protects the animal as his armour protected a medieval soldier and it helps to prevent water loss from the body by evaporation. In insect the thinner and more flexible parts of the skeleton consist of a watertight substance called chitin, the thicker and rigid parts of sclerotin. There is, however, a serious disadvantage in having one's skeleton outside. Since it is not surrounded by living tissue, as our bones are, it cannot grow. For this reason insects have to shed their outer covering at intervals. When this is done a new skin has always already formed underneath, and it is soft at first and stretches easily, allowing for rapid growth. But it soon hardens and further growth must wait for the next moult, or ecdysis as it is correctly called. Ecdysis is a serious hazard in insects' lives; they are helpless and vulnerable just before, during and just after it.

The life history of every insect consists of a succession of these ecdyses. The simplest sort of life history is illustrated by the silverfish (*Lepisma*), a little wingless insect found living in houses in most parts of the world. The female lays eggs from which hatch tiny individuals that differ from their parents only in size. These feed, as the adults do, on any starchy or sugary substances they can find, and they grow, shedding their skins as they do so. When they reach a certain size they mate and lay eggs, and continue to grow and moult at intervals after they have started breeding. A silverfish may undergo as many as fifty ecdyses in the course of its lifetime.

The life history of a grasshopper is rather less simple. The hatchling is recognisably a grasshopper, but it has no wings. In the course of growing up it moults five to eight times, and after the first or second ecdysis the wings appear as little pads or flaps. With each successive moult they become larger relative to the size of the insect, until finally they are completely developed and the grasshopper can fly. It is now fully grown and ready to breed and it never moults again. The bugs (Hemiptera) have a similar type of life history. Almost all insects cease to moult when their wings are fully formed. The mayflies (Ephemeroptera) are the one exception: they moult once again after emerging from the water and developing their wings.

6

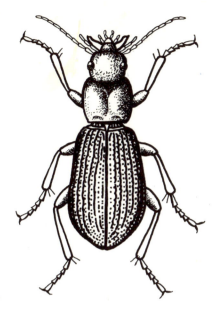

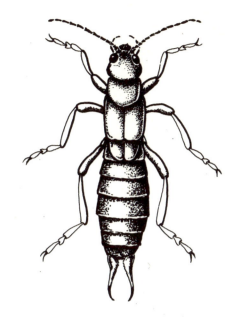

Butterflies afford a good example of the third type of insect life history. The little creature that emerges from a butterfly's egg is quite unlike a butterfly; it is more like a worm and we call it a caterpillar or larva. It feeds on leaves and grows rapidly; its skin is softer and more flexible than that of most insects, but it has to moult several times nevertheless. When it is ready for ecdysis the caterpillar spins a mat of silk on a leaf and fastens its rearmost legs to it. The skin behind the head splits and the insect crawls out, leaving its old covering anchored to the silken mat.

When it has completed its growth the caterpillar hangs itself up with threads of silk and remains without moving for a day or two. It then moults again, but this time there appears, not just another larger caterpillar, but a pupa or chrysalis having the form of a capsule without any limbs or appendages. While the larva was hanging up, and before the ecdysis, an extraordinary process took place: all its muscles and most of its internal organs dissolved into a kind of living soup, which then quickly reassembled to form a butterfly. The chrysalis is really a complete butterfly packed away in a hard envelope.

After a period of weeks or months the final ecdysis takes place; the shell of the pupa splits and the butterfly crawls out. At first its wings are like little crumpled bags. To expand them the insect pumps body fluid into them and then withdraws it, so that they flatten to form the broad patterned wings of the perfect insect. Take a new paper bag, crumple it into a ball without tearing it and then inflate it by blowing into it. Finally let the air out and flatten the bag into its original rectangular shape. This illustrates, with some simplification, how a butterfly expands its wings.

In this case there are three distinct stages, after hatching from the egg, which look like three quite different animals, and all three behave differently. The caterpillar climbs and crawls among foliage and devours leaves; the chrysalis cannot move about at all; and the butterfly flies in the air and feeds by sucking nectar from flowers through a long tube-like proboscis.

The changes of form that an insect undergoes in its lifetime are called metamorphoses. In the butterfly metamorphosis is said to be complete, in the grasshopper, incomplete. The silverfish grows up without metamorphosis. The kind of life history they undergo is an important point in classification of insects. In the list we have given the last four orders (Lepidoptera to Hymenoptera) have complete metamorphosis; in all the preceeding orders it is incomplete.

The time that insects take to complete their growth varies, but in general the warmer the climate the faster growth proceeds, and small insects grow up faster than large ones. In temperate climates life histories are related to the seasons and many of the butterflies have just one generation a year, but in the tropics they may develop from egg to perfect insect in three weeks or so, and breeding is continuous. In northern regions near the Arctic Circle many insects take two years to complete their life cycle. The North American Periodical Cicada, which lives underground during its early stages, takes as much as seventeen years to grow to full size. Even this is not a record; a kind of beetle, *Hylotrupes bajulus,* whose larva bores in wood, has been recorded as taking thirty-two years to grow up, though it normally completes its life history in a much shorter time.

How insects protect themselves

Freshwater fishes, frogs, lizards, the majority of small birds, practically all spiders and many kinds of insects hunt and devour insects unceasingly. The obvious reaction of the victims is to avoid being eaten if they can, and natural selection has produced innumerable adaptations in insects of all kinds to this end.

Many of them depend almost solely on their rate of reproduction to defeat the inroads made by their enemies' appetites. The aphids or plant lice swarm in millions throughout the summer without any attempt to defend or conceal themselves. They are eaten in millions, but they multiply at such a rate that the best efforts of their foes make little impression on their numbers. This must also be

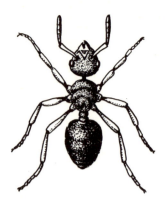

The bodies of insects take many different forms, from the practical robustness of the worker ant (above) to the attenuated grace of the crane fly (far right).

true of the tiny soil insects called springtails, whose incidence at 2½ millions per acre in grassland has already been referred to.

Among the larger insects, which do not exist in such huge numbers, we find more positive adaptations for protection. Most of them rely on concealment for safety, and many of these simply hide away in dark secret places where they are hard to see. This is specially true of insects which are active only at night and rest by day; many of the night-flying moths spend the daytime among thick foliage or in grass close to the ground. Other moths rest in the open on tree-trunks, and these always have colours and patterns that provide camouflage on their chosen backgrounds and make them almost invisible. Some are brown or gray, simulating bark; others have intricate markings of black and green so that they are concealed on a background of lichen.

Butterflies fly by day, but need to be concealed when they are resting, especially if they hibernate as butterflies through the winter. The European Anglewing or Comma (*Polygonis c-album*) spends the winter fast asleep in a bush or hedgerow. With its wings closed over its back (plate 48) its coloration and irregular outline give it an appearance so much like a tattered dead leaf that it has a good chance of escaping the hungry hunting birds that must find insects in the hardest winter or die of starvation. The famous Indian Leaf butterfly (*Kallima*, plate 49) even more perfectly simulates a dry brown leaf, even the midrib being represented by a dark line traversing both fore and hind wings. Both these butterflies are brightly coloured on the upper side of the wings and conspicuous when they fly or rest with the wings expanded.

The Buff-tip moth (*Phalera bucephala*, plate 38) has a shape and pattern by which it resembles a broken twig when it is at rest. The wings are mottled grey, like dead bark, and their yellowish tips are held together in such a way that they look like the wood that is exposed at the end of a snapped twig. The front of the thorax is also yellow.

In their early stages, when they have no means of escape by flight, butterflies and moths are in even greater need of

protection from their enemies. Many caterpillars are coloured green to blend with the foliage among which they live. Others have an amazingly exact resemblance to twigs. When they are at rest they complete the effect by adopting a special posture, holding on with the hindmost legs and stretching the body out straight and motionless.

The pupae of those moths whose larvae burrow into the ground to pupate are, of course, wholly concealed from predators that hunt by sight, but they are heavily preyed on by moles, which must play a large part in keeping these insects' numbers down to a safe level. The caterpillar of the Puss moth (*Dicranura vinula*, plate 37) pupates in a cocoon spun on the bark of the poplar or willow tree on whose leaves it fed. The cocoon not only resembles the bark, so that it is difficult to see, but is so hard that few birds can peck it open even if they find it.

Large insects have more difficulty in concealing themselves than small ones, and those that fly only feebly or not at all stand in most need of concealment. It is perhaps for these reasons that the stick-insects and leaf-insects (*Phasmida*, plates 10, 11) afford some of the most impressive instances of natural camouflage known. Their attenuated bodies and legs, combined with suitable coloration, are enough to disguise the stick-insects, but the adaptations of leaf-insects (which are all found in the tropics) are quite extraordinary. Their bodies are flattened and they often have flat outgrowths on their legs, and are usually green with markings closely resembling the network of veins in a leaf; sometimes they also have markings just like the blemishes that appear on leaves that are injured or attacked by fungi.

Not all insects, of course, need to hide in order to protect themselves. Bees and wasps have venomous stings and most predators leave them alone. A wasp pecked by a bird, however, will die of its injuries even if it manages to inflict a sting and so cause the bird to release it. For this reason most insects armed in this way, far from being camouflaged, are conspicuously coloured, often with black and yellow or red stripes. This is known as warning coloration and it enables birds to recognise dangerous

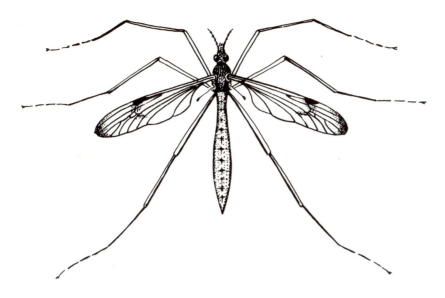

insects after one or two encounters and to avoid them. Although a few individual wasps may be sacrificed, the species as a whole gains protection.

A great many insects are protected against predation not by possession of a weapon but by evil-smelling, ill-tasting or even poisonous body fluids. It is a matter of common experience that many bugs smell unpleasant, especially if molested or injured, and most of the species with this property are vividly coloured, often black and red. Two examples are on plates 22 and 23. Many moths and butterflies, too, have a nauseous taste and are avoided by birds that have learned to recognise them. Frequently the larvae of these insects feed on plants which have bitter or poisonous sap. This is true of the butterflies of the family Danaidae, of which the well known Monarch is an example. Its caterpillar feeds on milkweed (*Asclepias*) which has a poisonous and ill-tasting juice, and the insect retains the essence of this throughout all its stages. In addition the larvae are protected from accidental destruction by grazing animals because they avoid feeding on the milkweed.

Every bird has to learn by experience that the Monarch butterflies are inedible. In this connection it is interesting to note that Monarchs (and other Danaid butterflies as well) are remarkably tough and leathery and can accept very rough treatment without being disabled or injured. A bird may capture one of these butterflies, peck it and so become aware of its nasty taste, and then drop it, and the insect will usually fly away unhurt. Bodily toughness of this kind would be of little use to an edible butterfly; its suffering in the course of being dismembered and eaten would merely be prolonged. But to the Danaids, which have a good chance of being released soon after they are caught, it is of definite survival value.

The caterpillars of many moths, including the familiar tiger moths of Europe and North America, have a coating of hairs which has earned them the name of 'woolly bears', and which undoubtedly gives them protection against being eaten. In the processionary moths (*Thaumetopoea,* plate 34) some of the hairs are poisonous and cause acute urticaria of the human skin, and are dangerous if they get into the eyes

or respiratory passages. Another moth with larvae of this type is the Brown-tail *(Euproctis phaeorrhoea),* a European species that was accidentally introduced into the U.S.A. about the end of the last century.

Many kinds of wasps, as we have seen, advertise their dangerous nature by a pattern of black and yellow stripes. Insects of other orders, wholly unrelated to wasps, are often found with coloration of this kind, but lacking in any genuine defence against predation – they are neither dangerous nor ill-tasting. Good examples of this are found among flower flies (*Syrphidae,* plate 53), some of which are striped like wasps, others furry, resembling bees. There is little doubt that such insects gain protection against birds from this sort of false warning coloration, and the term mimicry is used to define resemblances of this kind. A beetle which is probably a wasp mimic is shown on plate 86.

There is a species of flower fly, the Drone fly (*Eristalis tenax*) which resembles a honeybee so closely that mankind was deceived for hundreds of years. These flies will lay their eggs, and the larvae will feed, in a rotting carcass, and eventually a swarm of flies will hatch from its remains. This gave rise to the curious myth that an animal carcass, left to putrefy, will generate a swarm of bees. The belief persisted from the dawn of history right up to the 17th century, and we encounter it in the Old Testament story of Samson and the lion and the riddle. 'out of the strong came forth sweetness'. Although a drone fly looks very like a bee a moment's examination of it will reveal that it has only one pair of wings (a bee has two), that it cannot sting and, of course, it never produces any honey. It is extraordinary that the belief should have persisted so long when its falsity could be so easily demonstrated.

Distasteful butterflies are often mimicked with remarkable exactness by unrelated species which are really edible. In North America the Monarch (*Danaus plexippus*) is mimicked by a butterfly of the family Nymphalidae, the Viceroy (*Limenitis archippus*). Experiments have been made in which captive scrub jays were given various edible butterflies, including Viceroys, and ate them readily. Some of the birds were then given Monarchs, of which they

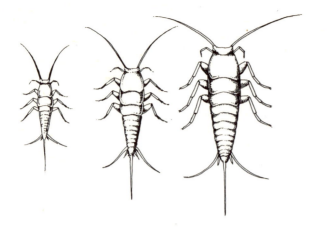
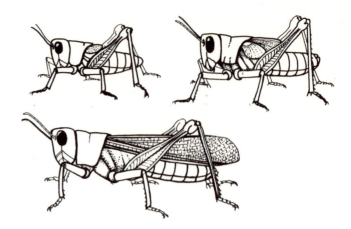

The life-history of every insect is a series of ecdyses. That of the silverfish is the simplest of all – it simply moults its skin as it grows – but a grasshopper changes the form of its wings at each moult. The shield bug is similar; but the butterfly has three distinct stages of metamorphosis.

pecked, or even ate, one or two, and then rejected them on sight. If these jays, which had experienced the unpleasant consequences of attacking a Monarch, were then offered Viceroys, they rejected them, and their resemblance to the Monarch is the only explanation for this.

Wings and flight

Insects learned to fly in the evolutionary sense long before any other group of animals. The earliest fossil of a winged insect dates from the Devonian period of geology, over 350 million years ago, long before the time of the dinosaurs, in fact before the vertebrate animals had got beyond the state of being fishes. The insect was a cockroach-like creature and has received the appropriate name of *Eopterum* or 'dawn-wing'. In the following period, the Carboniferous, which ended 280 million years ago, a variety of winged insects already existed, including dragonflies, mayflies and cockroaches. Some of the dragonflies had a wing-span of over two feet and are the largest of all known insects.

The wings of birds, bats and the extinct pterodactyls are limbs which were primarily developed for running and became modified as organs of flight. Insects' wings do not have this sort of origin. They probably first arose as lateral expansions from the thorax and became enlarged to form gliding planes in certain insects which took to jumping as a mode of progression. Later they acquired basal articulations and muscles and evolved into wings.

The wing of an insect is formed of two very thin and often transparent layers of chitin. When it is fully developed these are closely adherent and appear as a single sheet, but the layers can readily be separated in an insect that has just emerged from the pupa. The wing is strengthened by a framework of hollow rods, usually called the veins. Although they play the part of blood vessels during the growth of the wing, their main function is to stiffen and support it when it is fully developed.

The arrangement of the veins in the wing is not just a haphazard network. It is constant for each species and the

different orders usually show characteristic features in the venation, which are of importance in the classification. One interesting reason why the wing venation is such a valuable feature in classification is that the wings of insects are more often found in a good state of preservation as fossils than any other part of them. In fine-grained sediments such as shale, imprints of wings, flattened between the layers, may give a picture of the arrangement of the veins almost as complete and clear as that shown by the wing of a fly or a bee mounted on a microscope slide. The evolution of wing venation can therefore be studied in detail, not only by reference to living types, but through the geological record as well.

Studies based on this sort of evidence have enabled entomologists to establish a hypothetical primitive wing-type, in which the veins and their branches are given names or numbers. The venation of all the orders of winged insects can be referred to this system of notation. The most primitive type of insect wing is that represented today by the mayflies and dragonflies. In this type the main longitudinal veins are joined by a close network of cross-veins. The tendency in evolution has been towards reduction in the number of veins, especially the cross-veins, and towards thickening and strengthening of those which remain, and these become thickened and lie close together at and near the front margin. This strengthens the front or leading edge of the wing, which is the part that bears the greatest stress in flight.

Most flying insects have two pairs of wings, but in some the front pair serve as a protective covering for the hind wings rather than as organs of flight. This is the case in beetles, grasshoppers and their allies (Orthoptera) and in some of the bugs (Hemiptera). In the most advanced four-winged insects, the butterflies and moths (Lepidoptera) and the bees and wasps (Hymenoptera) the fore and hind wings are usually coupled together so that they work in unison. In the Hymenoptera a row of minute hooks along the leading edge of the hind wing engage in a fold at the rear edge of the fore wing. Flies have only a single pair, the hind wings having become transformed to

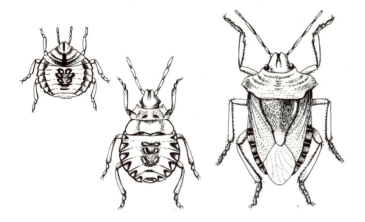

little knobbed stalks called halteres (plate 52). These vibrate with the same frequency as the wings and are believed to act as gyroscopic balancing organs.

An insect's wings work by flapping up and down, at the same time twisting at the base in such a way that the leading edge is below the hinder edge on the down-stroke and above it on the up-stroke. The effect of this is to fan a stream of air downwards and backwards, driving the insect forwards and supporting it against the pull of gravity. Power may be applied to the wings in one of two ways. Muscles in the thorax may be attached to the base of the wings and move them up and down. These are called direct wing muscles and are important in dragonflies, grasshoppers, cockroaches and beetles. In the more advanced insects movement is effected by indirect wing muscles which are attached only to the inner surfaces of the thorax, not to the wings themselves. When the vertical indirect muscles contract they pull down the roof of the thorax and this has the effect of lifting the wings upwards, owing to the peculiar way in which they are hinged to the sides of the thorax. Contraction of the longitudinal indirect muscles, which run from the front to the back of the thorax, causes the roof to bulge upwards and the wings to perform a downward stroke.

The wings beat at widely varying rates in different insects. In butterflies the rate is eight to twelve complete up-and-down strokes per second. In large moths it is fifty to seventy, in the housefly 200 and the surprising figure of over 1,000 beats per second has been established for a small midge called *Forcipomyia*.

The speed at which insects fly is difficult to estimate and is often exaggerated. The truth is that they cannot fly very fast. Horseflies (plates 50, 51) have been observed to keep up with vehicles travelling at 25 to 30 mph. Presumably they mistake them for large animals of some kind. A maximum speed of 36 mph has been calculated from observations on a large Australian dragonfly, and this is the highest speed definitely known to be attained by an insect.

On the other hand insects which have the urge to migrate may cover great distances, the larger ones by their own motive power, the smaller usually assisted by wind. A Monarch butterfly, marked in Ontario in August 1957, was recovered in January 1958 in Mexico at a distance of 1,870 miles. This was only the insect's southward flight, performed at the approach of winter. In the spring individuals which have migrated from the north in the previous fall perform a northward journey, and a distance of 600 miles for this has been proved by a similar mark-release-recover experiment. It must be supposed therefore that some Monarch butterflies travel over 2,000 miles in the course of their lives.

A very long journey by a small moth was established in a dramatic way in England in 1960. On 10 March of that year a specimen of *Nomophila noctuella* was captured and found to contain a radioactive particle that could be identified as a fallout product of the French nuclear bomb exploded in the Sahara on 13 February. All the evidence indicated that the particle had been taken up by the moth in North Africa and that it had therefore flown some 1,500 miles.

Senses of insects

Insects communicate with each other and keep in touch with the world around them by seeing, hearing and smelling, just as the more familiar animals do, but their sense organs are very different from our own. In those where the sense of sight is important the eyes are of the type known as compound and consist of a large number of identical units, each of which contains a lens. These units appear on the surface of the eye as tiny facets and can easily be seen if the eye of a suitable insect is examined under magnification. The picture of a wasp's face on plate 110 shows them clearly. In dragonflies, which have the largest eyes of any insects, there may be as many as 28,000 units in each eye. Each unit registers the intensity of light from a narrow direction, and a picture of the insect's surroundings is built up in terms of a large number of dots of greater or less brightness. The principle is similar to that used in reproducing a photograph in a newspaper by half-tone printing. Eyes of this kind must produce less accurate and

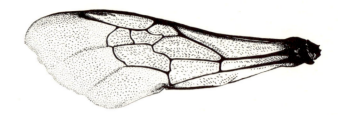

The primitive wing type of the damsel fly (left) with its close network of veins; and the highly-developed wing of the bumblebee, with its strengthened leading edge.

detailed images than human eyes, but they are very efficient at detecting movement. Butterflies need to be stalked with great care and a dragonfly may be startled by a sudden movement as much as forty feet away.

The sense of smell is located in the antennae and is the dominant sense in many insects. The antennae intercept scent molecules carried on the air or may be used as feelers to touch and test objects that the insect encounters. Ants certainly use their antennae in both these ways, and they communicate by touching and stroking each other with their antennae. Moths and butterflies when laying their eggs find the particular plants which will correctly nourish their caterpillar offspring by their sense of smell. Female moths usually emit an attractive scent when they are ready to mate and the males often have the antennae branched like a fine comb with two rows of teeth. The effect of this is to present a large surface to the air and so pick up scent molecules as efficiently as possible.

Some butterflies have a delicate sense of taste located on the fore feet. The Red Admiral (*Vanessa atalanta*) can distinguish by touching with its fore feet between distilled water and a solution of sugar 1/200 of the strength of the most dilute solution perceptible to the human tongue.

Only a few insects have identifiable organs of hearing and most of these are types that communicate with each other by sound. These ears, or tympanal organs, may be located on the body or legs, but are never where we might expect them, on the head. Each such organ consists of a small pit in the chitin of the external skeleton with a stretched membrane, a sort of eardrum, at the bottom of it. In short-horned grasshoppers and locusts the tympanal organs are at the base of the abdomen, close to where it joins the thorax, but in crickets and the long-horned grasshoppers or bush-crickets they are near the base of the tarsi or end joints of the fore legs, so that these insects can be said to listen with their wrists. In cicadas the 'ears' are in a cavity in the same part of the body as the sound-producing organs.

Most sound production by insects forms part of the courtship between the sexes. Usually the male calls to the female, both to enable her to locate him and to stimulate her inclination for mating. His song also has the effect of warning other males to keep away from his territory. To be effective the 'songs' must be individual for each species, and indeed they are so; some kinds of crickets are more easily identified by their voices than by any features that can be examined in a preserved specimen. Sound recordings of the songs of male crickets will cause obvious excitement in females, but only in those of the same species.

The method of producing the sounds is usually that known as stridulation in which a ridge is drawn over a row of closely spaced points or tubercles. The size and spacing of these determines the song in much the same way as the formations in the groove on a gramophone record determine the sound production. The insects produce their sounds by moving one part of the body against another, and the combinations vary from one group to another. In the grasshoppers the inner surface of the largest joint or femur of the hind leg has a row of fine points which are drawn across a ridge on the fore wing. Bush-crickets and crickets carry a ridge on one of the thick, leathery fore wings and a row of points on the other, and stridulate by rubbing the wings against each other.

Cicadas have the loudest voices of all insects and a method of voice production that is quite peculiar to them. In a cavity at the base of the abdomen there is a pair of tightly stretched membranes and special muscles cause these to vibrate. The cavity acts as a resonator and the noise made by some of the big tropical cicadas seems almost deafening to human ears at close quarters.

Some kinds of night-flying moths have tympanal organs on their bodies but do not communicate with each other vocally, so that the purpose of their sense of hearing is far from obvious. It now seems certain that it has been developed as a defence against bats, which are the most serious enemies that adult moths have to contend with. It is well known that bats avoid obstacles and locate flying prey by emitting very high pitched (ultrasonic) sounds which are reflected as echoes from any object in the animal's vicinity.

'Stick' caterpillars (above), which can raise their bodies to look like young twigs; and (right) the handsome Tiger moth.

The bat locates and identifies the object by interpreting these echoes, just as radar interprets echoes of radio pulses reflected from ships or aircraft.

Research has shown that the hearing organs of moths are sensitive to ultrasonic vibrations of just the same frequencies as those emitted by hunting bats. Vibrations of this kind, even when produced artificially, cause moths at which they are directed to dodge erratically or to close their wings and fall to the ground. One group of tropical American moths have carried defensive measures further still. They themselves emit ultrasonic vibrations which are believed to 'jam' the sound-radar of their enemies.

Social insects

A nest of wasps or yellowjackets at the height of the summer may have a population of 5,000 individuals, and as many as 25,000 may live in the nest and die in the course of a season. If the nest is attacked or threatened they will fly out to defend it with their stings, and with no regard at all for their individual lives, and for as long as they live their energies are devoted to the maintenance of the nest and to feeding and caring for thousands of larvae. As soon as these mature and can fly they engage in the same selfless communal service, dying after a few weeks, but constantly replaced until the first frosts of the fall put an end to their community and to the lives of all but a few specially endowed females which will hibernate through the winter. Such communities are often compared with cities or states under totalitarian rule, but this analogy loses sight of the fact they they are *families*. Almost all of them are sisters, female offspring of the single mother or 'queen'; a few males are present towards the end of the season, but in the history of the nest only the single queen produces any offspring.

This history is briefly as follows. In the spring queen wasps emerge from hibernation and construct small nests of a kind of papery material made from a paste of chewed-up wood. The nest may be suspended from a branch above ground or from a root intersecting a mouse-hole. The queen has mated the previous fall and has a store of living sperm in a sac in her body called a spermatheca. She constructs a number of cells in the nest, opening downwards, and lays in each an egg fertilised by a single sperm from her store. The eggs hatch and she rears the larvae to full size, feeding them on chewed fragments of flies and caterpillars. After a brief period as pupae these produce wasps, rather small and all females. These daughters of the queen fly out and collect food for the fresh generation of larvae that is growing up in the nest, and make fresh paper to enlarge it. If it is underground they bite away the earth to enlarge the cavity, carrying the spoil outside. As the population increases so does the volume of work that can be done, and the nest becomes large and populous. The queen no longer goes out but stays at home, fertilizing and laying thousands of eggs, singly in cells made by her teeming daughters. Although they are females they live and die without ever meeting a male or (with rare exceptions) ever laying an egg. These are the individuals commonly known as 'workers', and the name is well earned. Near the end of the summer individuals of two different kinds appear, queens and males. The queens arise, just as workers do, from fertilised eggs, and it is not known how it is determined that an egg shall produce a queen, which is larger than the workers and endowed with the instinct and capacity for reproduction. The males are produced in a most peculiar way: the queen simply withholds the usual fertilising sperm when laying the egg, and the larvae that hatch from such unfertilised eggs develop into males. The occasional eggs laid by workers produce males in the same way. These reproductively competent individuals of both sexes leave the nest and fly away, and the queens mate, hibernate and found new nests in the following year.

Two other groups of the same order, the Hymenoptera, show the same pattern of living and breeding, the bees and the ants. Not all bees (nor all wasps) are social insects, in fact only a small minority of the species are so. The others, the so-called solitary wasps and bees, make nests for their young and provision them with food for the larvae, but the

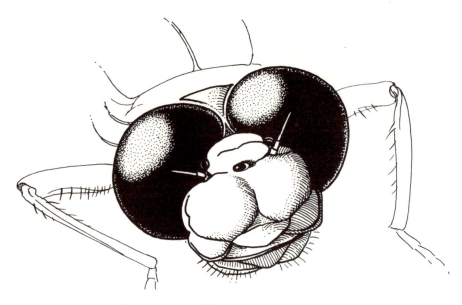

Dragonflies have the largest eyes of any insect, with as many as 28,000 units in each eye.

females do this unaided by any worker caste of non-reproductive individuals. All wasps, social or otherwise, feed their young on insects and other small animals such as spiders. All bees subsist throughout their lives on honey and pollen from flowers.

All ants are social insects, living in communities with non-reproductive female workers. Their habits and food preferences are various and they perform such quasi-human activities as keeping other insects, such as aphids, as domestic animals and making slaves of other species of ants. Their colonies may be enormous, containing half a million or more individuals. Worker ants are always wingless; the queens and males have wings, but the queens break theirs off after mating and before founding their nests. Bees and ants produce females and males respectively from fertilised and unfertilised eggs, just as wasps do.

The other social insects are the termites, often misleadingly called 'white ants'. They form a separate order, the Isoptera, and are quite unrelated to ants. Their nearest relatives among the other insects are the cockroaches. In many ways their colonies and habits parallel those of ants, but they differ in having incomplete metamorphosis, so that their newly hatched young are very like the adults, except for size, and active from the beginning of their lives. Also the workers are of both sexes and the nests are populated by a 'royal couple', a king and a huge swollen queen, which live together, mating at intervals. A queen termite has been seen to lay 36,000 eggs in 24 hours, and colonies may number several millions. Termites live on vegetable matter; some feed on dead wood and are destructive of timber used in building.

Men and insects

It is unfortunately true that we have more enemies among the insects than friends, but it is also true that the vast majority are completely neutral in the context of human interests. Harmful insects fall under three main headings. First they may be the cause of direct discomfort and,

rarely, danger. The sting of many kinds of wasps and hornets is very painful and people occasionally die from multiple stings. The Asian Giant Honeybee is another insect that sometimes causes casualties in this way if its enormous hanging combs are disturbed. Mosquitoes and other blood-sucking flies may cause distress if they are present in great numbers. In the brief summer of the Arctic tundra special clothing, including a veil to protect the head and face, is needed to keep off mosquitoes.

Far more important are the insect carriers of disease. Most of these are blood-suckers which pierce the skin of men and other animals in order to feed. Invariably they inject a fluid to prevent the blood clotting in their slender, syringe-like mouthparts and feed by sucking up blood only after this is done. If they have already bitten a person harbouring the disease he will be infected with the parasitic organisms causing it. These will be introduced into the blood of the victim and, of course, not all sucked back again. In such cases certain insects are almost always associated specifically with certain diseases and the life history of the parasite requires an alternation between the two hosts. The parasite that causes malaria is introduced into the human blood stream by the bite of mosquitoes of a certain genus, *Anopheles*. It cannot pass the insect-borne phase of its life history in any other host and malaria is contracted through being bitten by an *Anopheles* mosquito which has previously bitten a person suffering from the disease. A similar relationship exists between man, mosquitoes of another genus, *Aedes,* and the virus of yellow fever, but the virus can also live in the blood of monkeys. The bacillus of plague is transmitted by the bite of fleas which normally live on rats, but leave the animals when they die of the disease and resort to biting humans if they cannot gain access to another rat. The Tsetse fly of Africa conveys an organism called a trypanosome which causes the terrible human disease sleeping sickness and also the devastating cattle disease nagana. Tsetse flies will feed on the blood of any animal, but those animals that are native to Africa, such as antelopes, are immune to the disease. Houseflies carry intestinal infections such as

The feathery antennae of a male moth can detect the scent of a female from a considerable distance.

dysentery and cholera simply by feeding on crude sewage and then on exposed human food. Here no elaborate life history of the parasite is involved, it is merely carried on the fly's mouthparts. This catalogue of insect-borne disease could be extended, but enough has been said to show how serious the problem is.

The third type of insect enemy is the one which attacks the plants that form the basis of agriculture. As an example of these it is instructive to look at the history of the Colorado beetle (plate 90). It was discovered in 1823 in the Rocky Mountains, feeding on a plant called buffalo burr and doing no harm at all. Potato is allied to buffalo burr and acceptable to the beetle as food. When potatoes came to be grown over areas covering hundreds of square miles it transferred its attention to them. Being provided with a limitless food supply it multiplied prodigiously. Every major crop pest has a similar history and is a product of the intensive agriculture that accompanies civilisation.

We must wage war against insects that menace our health and well-being, and the case for making it total war, aimed at extermination, seems difficult to dispute. But total war of any kind, backed by the weapons of modern science, involves risks of disaster not only for the enemy but for neutrals and for the wielders of such weapons themselves. Modern pesticides contribute seriously to the destruction of wild life of all kinds and are progressively poisoning the land and fresh waters and even the oceans. They are present in the bodies of every one of us and their use must be curtailed if they are not to reach levels that affect our health and that of our children.

It is pleasant to turn away from this sombre picture and end on a more pleasant theme, that of our insect friends and allies. Mention has been made in our foreword of the enlisting of predatory insects against others which have become pests, or against plants which run wild as uncontrollable weeds. This is known as biological control and is resorted to, in preference to pesticides, wherever possible.

There are also insects which are actually domesticated, like the Silk Moth (*Bombyx mori,* plate 40), which is believed to have been first used by the Chinese to produce silk about 4,000 years ago. Honeybees also have a long history of domestication. The bee keepers of ancient Egypt put their hives on boats in the spring and drifted slowly northward down the Nile, following the first opening of the flowers.

In recent years Professor W. P. Stephen of Oregon State University has pioneered work on the pollination of alfalfa. Honeybees do not do this effectively, and it was known that small solitary bees are its chief pollinators. Unfortunately intensive agriculture discourages the natural breeding of these, so that wherever alfalfa was grown on a large scale it set very little seed. Professor Stephen found two kinds of these bees which could be cultured artificially. For the Alkali bee (*Nomia melanderi*), which burrows in moist and slightly saline soil, he made 'bee beds' which matched their natural requirements, and soon had them breeding at a density of over 1,000 burrows to the square yard. The other is a species of Leaf-Cutter bee (*Megachile)* and it nests in hollow plant stems and similar situations. After a lot of experiment and hard work it was found that cartons of drinking straws, with their open ends exposed, were accepted as nesting sites by this bee.

In the past 175 to 200 pounds per acre has been an average figure for the production of alfalfa seed in the USA. Where the little solitary bees are cultured the figure has been increased to 1,600 and even 2,000 pounds. Work on these lines, with various kinds of bees and various crops as its object, is now being undertaken all over the world.

Dytiscus marginalis, life size.

2

3

4

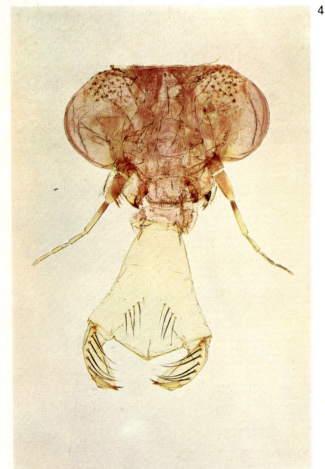

1 Beetles. End joint of the fore leg of a male diving beetle, *Dytiscus marginalis,* under strong magnification. The beetle is shown above at life size. The joint consists of an adhesive disk armed with numerous suckers, and it is used to hold the female during mating and also to cling to submerged objects. These beetles are predatory, both as larvae and adults, feeding on small fish, tadpoles and other aquatic insects. The beetles fly at night, so larvae may appear in ornamental ponds and fish hatcheries, where they can do serious harm.

2 Mayflies. These are delicate insects and are usually found near water, as their larvae are aquatic. The scientific name of the order, Ephemeroptera, implies that they live only for a day, and the winged flies are indeed very short lived and take no food at all. They are unique among insects in that, after they have left the water and developed their wings, they undergo a further moult. Mayflies are favourite food of fish, especially trout, and anglers have names for the various species and model their artificial flies on them.

3–4 Dragonflies and damselflies. These insects are all included in the order Odonata. The dragonflies are strong and swift-flying and rest with their wings extended on each side, damselflies are more delicate and rest with the wings held over the back. *Lestes virens* (3) is a damselfly. All the Odonata are predatory, both as adults and larvae. The adults have very large eyes and hunt by sight, catching insects on the wing and chewing them up with their powerful jaws. The larvae are all aquatic and have the lower lip or labium extensible and adapted for catching prey. It is generally carried folded under the head but can be shot out in front in order to seize a victim. A microscope preparation of the head of a dragonfly larva is shown (4) with the labium extended and the pair of grasping claws at the end of it is clearly seen. The larvae feed on small fish and anything else they can overpower.

5

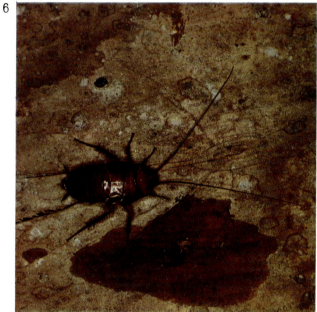

6

7

5, 6, 7 Cockroaches. The most familiar cockroaches are those which live in our houses and have been carried all over the world by shipping. The common cockroach, *Blatta orientalis,* is probably a native of Africa and can only live in heated buildings in temperate climates. The so-called American cockroach, *Periplaneta americana,* is the largest of the domestic cockroaches, growing to 1½ inches in length. Its name is misleading and it is probably also of African origin. In the tropics numerous species of cockroaches live in the wild state; some of them are very large insects. *Blabera gigantea* (5) is shown at actual size on this page. The eggs are enclosed in a capsule of chitin which is divided into a number of compartments, one for each egg. These capsules are called oothecae, and two are shown here (7).

9

8

8–9 Mantises. Nearly all mantises are tropical, a few species extending into warm-temperate regions. They are large insects and they walk on four legs, the fore legs being adapted for catching and holding prey; all mantises are predators, feeding on other insects. They do not pursue their victims but lie in wait for them, and their attitude when doing so, with the fore legs raised as if in supplication, has led to the name 'praying mantis'; the word 'mantis' means a prophet or soothsayer. Most of them are camouflaged, both to protect them from birds and to aid them in ambushing victims. They may be disguised as twigs or dead leaves (8), green leaves (9) or even as flowers. The eggs are enclosed in an ootheca, as in cockroaches, to which they are closely allied.

10–11 Stick-insects and leaf-insects, Phasmida. These insects afford some of the most impressive cases of natural camouflage that are known. The stick-insects have straight, usually extremely slender bodies and long legs, so that they look like twigs. *Dixippus appetens* (10) is one of these. The eggs are simply dropped on the ground. A common species of the eastern United States, *Diapheromera femorata,* sometimes builds up to such numbers that the noise of the eggs dropping sounds like falling rain. Leaf-insects such as *Phyllium* (11) are elaborately adapted to look like leaves, veins and blemishes of the leaf all being accurately simulated.

10

11

12

13

14

12, 13, 14 Grasshoppers. Three species are illustrated, *Gomphocerus sibiricus*, *Arcyptera fusca* and *Paracinema lineatus*. They have the hind legs greatly enlarged for jumping and most of them can fly as well. Some kinds of large grasshoppers occur occasionally in enormous swarms which migrate over great distances and do very serious damage by devouring every scrap of vegetation that they encounter. These are known as locusts. Most of the species that occur in Africa and Asia have localized breeding grounds called 'outbreak areas', which are well known, and swarms can be destroyed at their source before they build up to great numbers. The desert locust, *Schistocerca gregaria*, however, still presents a serious international problem. It inhabits a great area from North Africa east to India and Pakistan, and large-scale breeding of it may occur in any suitable locality.

15–16 Earwigs. The chief characteristic of these insects is the pair of pincers or forceps at the hinder end. They are used in self defence, but are not very effective. Some, including the common European earwig, *Forficula auricularia,* have strong maternal instincts. The female lays about twenty eggs under a log or stone and guards them until they hatch, and she continues to look after the young for some time after hatching. This earwig has been introduced into the United States. Two species are illustrated, *Anechura bipunctata* and *Labidura riparia.* The latter, a rather large reddish-brown earwig, is usually found near the shore.

15

16

17 The Hemiptera or true bugs are divided into two suborders, Heteroptera and Homoptera. Of the former the bedbug, *Cimex lectularius,* is the most notorious. It lives in crevices in the interior of houses and of furniture and comes out at night to suck the blood of people when they are asleep. The bite is unpleasant and irritating and the bugs themselves have a disgusting smell. They can be killed with insecticides and by fumigation but are difficult to eradicate completely. The nearest relatives of the bedbug are parasites of bats, and this species probably transferred itself to man in the Stone Age, when men lived in bat-haunted caves.

18–19 All bugs feed by sucking the sap of plants or the blood of animals by means of a hollow piercing beak. This can be seen clearly in the African species *Platymerus guttatipennis* (18) which is a predator and belongs to the family Reduviidae or 'assassin bugs'. Usually the beak is folded under the head when not in use (19). Both these bugs belong to the Heteroptera.

17

20–21 In the Heteroptera the fore wings are each divided into two parts. The basal part is thick, consisting of sclerotin, and acts as a protective cover for the hind wings. Towards its tip the fore wing is thin and membranous. This division can be clearly seen in *Raphigaster nebulosa* (20), but in the curiously shaped *Phyllomorpha lacinata* (21) the fore wings are scarcely visible.

20

21

22

23

22-23 Many of the Hemiptera-Heteroptera are brightly and, to our eyes, attractively coloured. Most of these vividly coloured species will be found to have a strong and unpleasant smell, if handled, due to a fluid which they emit when alarmed. This makes them inedible for birds, and their conspicuous colouration acts as a warning against trying to make a meal of them. These two species, *Tropidothorax leucapterus* and *Callidea bohemani* illustrate this principle of warning colouration very well.

24–25 In the other suborder of the Hemiptera, the Hemoptera, the fore wings are not divided into thickened and membranous portions, but are of uniform texture throughout. Aphids or greenfly are the most familiar of all the Homoptera and the largest of them are the cicadas, in which the two pairs of membranous wings are easily seen. *Phyllotropus fuscata* and *Cyphonia hirta* (24, 25) are tropical species belonging to the family Membracidae or treehoppers.

26

27

26–27 Two more members of the Membracidae, *Cyphonia clavata* and *Heteronotus tridens* are shown here. They are small insects (the thorns in both pictures give an idea of their size) and as in most members of this group, the front part of the thorax is greatly enlarged and extends backwards over the body. In the three species shown on this page this extension is grotesquely developed to form a figure of spheres and spines. It is impossible to say what purpose such outgrowths serve.

30

28, 29, 30 Here are three more treehoppers (Membracidae) with extraordinary backward extensions of the prothorax. They are *Ennya chrysura*, *Bocydium rufiglabrum* and *Heteronotus abbreviatus*. The last photograph shows very clearly how the dorsal ornamentation originates as an outgrowth of the thorax. Most of the Membracidae are tropical and South America is particularly rich in them.

31

32

31, 32 The ornamentation of the treehoppers on the last four pages is difficult to interpret as an adaptation of any kind, but that of *Umbonia spinosa* clearly simulates a thorn and so serves to deceive birds and other predators which might make a meal of the insect. For this reason members of the genus *Umbonia* are often called thorn-bugs. The scale-insects (Coccidae) are also Homoptera. In most species the males, which are winged, are seldom seen. The females are often degenerate, lacking legs, wings and eyes, and are always covered with a coating of wax, so that they do not look like insects at all. *Coccus hemisphaericus* (32) is a typical scale-insect and a good example of the appearance which has given these insects their name. It feeds on the sap of a variety of plants. Some scale-insects are serious pests, one of the worst being the Cottony Cushion Scale (*Icerya purchasi*) which threatened to destroy the citrus orchards of California, but was controlled by the importation of a ladybird beetle from Australia.

33 Beetles. A greatly magnified view of part of the antenna of a beetle, showing the articulated segments. Some beetles have antennae much longer than their bodies.

34, 35, 36 Butterflies and moths (Lepidoptera). The larvae of the processionary moth, *Thaumatopea pityocampa* (34) live communally in silk nests on pine trees, which they may damage severely. When they go out to feed they form a column or 'procession', following each other nose-to-tail. Their hairs are poisonous, causing urticaria of the skin and severe irritation of the eyes and respiratory passages. The pupae of butterflies (35) are almost always formed without any covering and often merely hang by the tail to a twig or other support. The larvae of moths spin silken cocoons when ready to pupate. The one shown (36) has been cut open before the pupa was formed.

37, 38, 39 The puss moth, *Dicranura vinula* (37) is a handsome grey moth whose larva lives on willow and poplar. The caterpillar can emit a spray of formic acid if disturbed. The buff-tip, *Phalera bucephala* (38), is coloured and shaped so that it looks like a piece of broken twig and is well concealed whether it sits on a tree or on the ground in woodland. The death's-head sphinx moth, *Acherontia atropos* (39), is an African and southern European species which owes its name to the skull-like markings on its thorax. It has the power of squeaking quite loudly by ejecting air through the proboscis.

40–41 The silk moth, *Bombyx mori* (40), may have been domesticated in China as much as 4,000 years ago. Its ancestor, living in the wild, is unknown and is probably extinct. If it was confined to China this may well have come about by the constant escaping of individuals whose genetic character had been altered by selective breeding. Such moths, mating with those in the wild, would cause the free-living stock to become less able to maintain themselves and escape from their enemies. The natural silk industry is now declining due to competition from artificial fibres. The Apollo butterfly, *Parnassius apollo* (41), is a beautiful insect that is found on mountain ranges from Europe to central Asia. A great number of species of *Parnassius* live in Eurasia and a few in North America, and almost all are inhabitants of mountains, except in the far north, where they are found at sea level. The larvae feed on plants of the stonecrop family and spin cocoons in which to pupate, no doubt as a protection against the cold.

43

42

42–43 The order Lepidoptera takes its name from the fact that the wings are covered with tiny overlapping scales of various colours, and the arrangement of these determines the beautiful patterns which adorn the wings of butterflies and moths. The scales may be simply pigmented, or they may have ultramicroscopic structures which break up the light and produce colours in the same way as a film of oil on water. This results in a play of changing colours over the wings, and is well shown in the lesser purple emperor, *Apatura ilia* (42). The oak eggar moth, *Lasiocampa quercus* (43), has normally pigmented scales.

44–45 The peacock butterfly, *Inachis io,* has the upper side of the wings beautifully ornamented with eye-like spots on a deep red ground. Its under side coloration is, by contrast, very dark and renders the insect extremely inconspicuous when it closes its wings. As it hibernates through the winter as a butterfly concealment is particularly necessary for it.

46

46, 47, 48   Like *Inachis io* these three species spend the winter as butterflies and the small tortoiseshell, *Aglais urticae* (46) often hibernates in houses. This species and the comma or European anglewing, *Polygonia c-album* (48) feed as larvae on nettles, but the food plant of the Camberwell beauty or mourning cloak, *Nymphalis antiopa* (47), which is found both in North America and Eurasia, is willow, birch and other forest trees.

47

49 Some of the tropical butterflies afford wonderful examples of protective form and coloration, and the famous Indian leaf butterfly, *Kallima,* is a classical example of this. The under side of the wings have just the colour and texture of a dead leaf, and the two wings together simulate the shape of a leaf perfectly, the short tail on the hind wings representing the stalk. This is not all: when the wings are held in the natural position of rest a dark line runs across them, coinciding where the hind wing overlaps the fore wing, and accurately simulating the midrib of the leaf.

50–51 The horseflies or Tabanidae often have large and beautifully coloured eyes. Those of *Tabanus bromius* (50) are particularly striking. Female horseflies are unpleasant insects as they live on the blood of mammals and man, piercing the skin with a sharp sucking beak. The males are harmless, feeding on sap, the nectar of flowers and sometimes pollen.

52, 53, 54 Flies. The fruit flies and vinegar flies of the genus *Drosophila* (52) are strongly attracted to the smell of fruit, wine and beer, and often attempt to share our food and drink if it is of this kind. They will find a piece of banana peel left outside on a hot day within an hour or less. They are small flies and the illustration on the opposite page is greatly magnified. *Drosophila* is chiefly famous, however, for the very important part it has played in genetical studies. It can be easily and rapidly bred in controlled artificial conditions, and it has only four chromosomes, an exceptionally low number, which simplifies genetical studies. A further advantage is that the chromosomes in its salivary glands are unusually large.

Volucella zonaria (53) is one of the flower flies or hover flies (Syrphidae). Its appearance recalls that of a wasp, and this is probably a case of protective mimicry. The larvae live as scavengers in the nests of wasps.

The housefly, *Musca domestica* (54) is a familiar nuisance and may be a dangerous pest in countries with low standards of hygiene owing to its habit of feeding on sewage and exposed food, flying from one to the other carrying germs of disease.

53

54

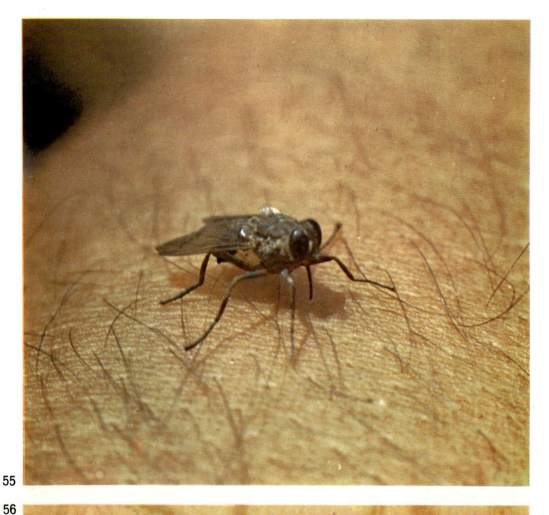

55

56

55, 56 Flies. The tsetse flies, *Glossinia palpalis*
and *Glossinia morsitans* are confined
to Africa, where they carry a protozoan parasite
called a trypanosome. The flies feed on the blood
of men and all kinds of animals. In man the
parasite causes the terrible disease of sleeping
sickness and in cattle the disease called nagana.
The native African animals harbour the parasite
in their blood but are immune to the disease. The
presence of tsetse flies makes the keeping of
horses and cattle impossible and is a serious
threat to human health. The flesh fly *Sarcophaga
carnaria* (56), does not lay eggs as most insects
do, but deposits larvae which have hatched from
eggs inside the fly's body. These are always
placed on exposed flesh, such as butcher's meat,
if this is not adequately protected. The larva
emits a digestive fluid which liquifies the flesh
and it then feeds on the resultant 'soup'.
Sometimes larvae are deposited on wounds of
animals or humans and they penetrate the
tissues, with serious results. Large numbers of
these larvae are artificially bred to serve as bait
for anglers.

57-58 Beetles. Typically these insects have mouthparts that include a pair of jaws or mandibles. These are sometimes developed to a remarkable degree as in the tropical species whose head, greatly magnified, is shown here (57). The tiger beetle, *Cicindela campestris* (58), owes its name to its habit of pursuing and devouring other insects, and it is equipped with a formidable pair of jaws for the purpose. Tiger beetles are found commonly in woods and heaths where the soil is sandy, and they run and fly so actively that they are difficult to capture. Their larvae live in burrows in the ground and are also predators.

57

58

48

59

60

59–63 The ground beetles (Carabidae) comprise a large number of species which are mostly active and predatory in their habits. The majority are coloured black or brown, like *Abax ater* (60), but some have brilliant metallic colours and are most beautiful insects, much sought after by collectors. Examples of these are *Carabus olympiae* (59), *Carabus solieri* (61) and *Carabus sycophanta* (62). The first of these was nearly exterminated by dealers, who captured them to sell to collectors all over the world. Most of the Carabid beetles have the wing-cases or elytra elegantly sculptured with longitudinal lines. *Allegretta boldorii* (63) lives in caves in southern Europe. Its powerful jaws are well shown in the photograph.

61

62

63

64

65

64–67 Beetles. The carrion beetles or sexton beetles include a number of species, some black, other conspicuously marked with black and orange, such as *Necrophorus vespilloides* (64). They have the habit of seeking out the dead bodies of small animals and burying them in the soil, thus fulfilling the function of a sexton or grave-digger. They feed on the decaying flesh and also lay their eggs on the body, which provides food for their larvae.

The rove beetles (Staphylinidae) are a very numerous group which have not the appearance of ordinary beetles because their wings and wing-cases do not extend to the hinder end of the body. Two species are shown, *Paederus fuscipes* (65) and *Staphylinus cesareus* (66). *Leptodirus hohenwarti* (67) is found only in caves. Its very long antennae and legs enable it to feel its way about in complete darkness. Many cave-dwelling insects are adapted in this way.

66

69

70

68, 69, 70 Beetles. One often finds among insects bodily structures which seem to be developed out of all proportion to the rest of the body. The well known stag beetle, *Lucanus cervus* (68) affords an example of this: the mandibles are enormous and branched, rather like the antlers of a stag. Only the male has this feature; in the female the mandibles are normally developed.

The scarab beetle shown on this page (69, 70) is not only brilliantly coloured, but has a long horn at the front of its head, recalling that of a rhinoceros. Many beetles of this family, the *Scarabaeidae,* have the habit of collecting the dung of animals, rolling it into a ball and then burying it to serve as provender for themselves and their young. One of the North African species was held in veneration by the ancient Egyptians, and it is represented frequently on their pottery and carved stone ornaments.

71

72

71–72   The heaviest and bulkiest insects in the world are included among the tropical members of the scarab family. *Dynastes hercules* (71), a native of tropical America, may attain to six inches in length, though a good part of this is taken up by the enormous forwardly directed horns on the head and thorax. The African Goliath beetle, *Goliathus giganteus* (72), is even more massive, with the body four inches long or more. Unlike most of the insects in this book the two on this page are shown on a reduced scale.

73 The rhinoceros beetle, *Oryctes nasicornis,* is a member of the scarab group found in Europe and North Africa; large specimens are about 1½ inches long. As in most of these fantastically developed scarab beetles the horns and other protuberances are seen only in the males. This beetle flies at night and sometimes blunders into houses. A larger species, *Oryctes rhinoceros,* is often a serious pest in coconut groves in eastern Asia. The beetles bore into the young shoots to feed on the sweet sap but their larvae live on decaying vegetable matter and do no harm.

74

74, 75, 76 Many kinds of beetles live among foliage and on flowers, where they can be searched for or collected by sweeping the vegetation with a strongly made net. Both the species on this page are lovers of flowers. They are *Hoplia coerulea* (74) and *Trichius fasciatus* (75). The latter is hairy and resembles a bumblebee, especially when in flight.

Some of the metallic wood-boring beetles (Buprestidae) are among the most brilliant of all insects. This is especially true of the tropical species, of which *Chrysochroa fulgidissima* (76) is an example from eastern Asia. Some kinds of these beautiful beetles are caught in large numbers to be made into ornaments. The larvae of all the Buprestids are borers in wood.

75

77, 78, 79 *Lampra rutilans* is another example of a beautifully coloured
Buprestid beetle from tropical forest. The Elateridae or click beetles are well known
from their ability, when turned on their backs, to jump in the air with a clicking
sound. If the beetle lands still upside-down it repeats the performance until it comes
down on its feet. The species shown here, *Ctenicera virens* (78), is remarkable for its
greatly developed branched antennae. The fireflies, *Pyrophorus,* of the Americas also
belong to this family of beetles.
Trichodes alvearius (79) feeds on pollen as a beetle, but has very different habits in
its larval stage. It then lives in the nests of bees, feeding on the honey and pollen
stored by its hosts and sometimes even devouring their larvae.

80-81 The bark beetles (Scolytidae) tunnel between the wood and the bark of trees, sometimes destroying the vital cambium or zone of growth in the outermost wood. In this way these minute beetles may be responsible for the death of a tree two hundred feet or more in height. In their burrowing the beetles make a characteristic pattern of grooves in the surface of the wood, and are sometimes called engraver beetles on this account. The pattern (80) is formed of a central gallery, made by the beetles themselves, often a couple, male and female. The lateral galleries are formed by the larvae which are their offspring.

On the other hand some beetles are our friends and allies. This is especially true of the ladybird beetles (Coccinellidae) many of which feed on aphids and scale-insects. *Hippodamia tredecimpunctata* (81) is one of these.

80

81

82 The darkling beetles (Tenebrionidae) are nocturnal in their habits and feed, both as larvae and adults, on vegetable material, especially dead and decaying wood and fungi of various kinds. The larvae (82) have a characteristic appearance and can easily be found under the bark of fallen trees. A very well known species is *Tenebrio molitor,* whose larva is known as the mealworm. These larvae will feed on any sort of dry cereal or bran and are exceedingly easy to rear. Much use is made of them for feeding captive insectivorous birds and reptiles, and also as a lure to tame birds in one's garden.

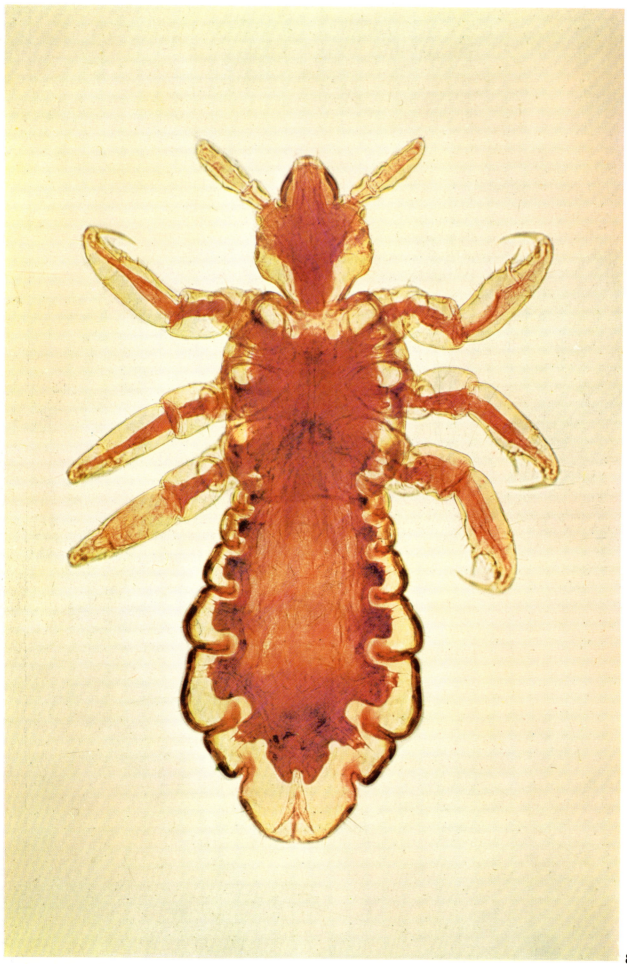

83 The common louse, *Pediculus humanus,* is shown as a microscope preparation.
It is a parasite of man and exists as two races or subspecies, the head louse, which
infests the hair of the head and the body louse which lives in the clothing that is worn
next to the skin. The eggs, known as 'nits', are glued firmly to the hair or fibres, and
the fore legs of the insects are adapted for holding very tightly to a hair, so that they
are difficult to dislodge. People living in crowded conditions with little chance to
wash or change their clothes are liable to become infested. The dangerous disease
called typhus is conveyed by lice. In the days when prisoners were closely confined
in very unhygienic conditions they were subject to terrible epidemics of typhus,
which came to be called 'jail fever'.

84 Beetles of the genus *Blaps* are often called churchyard beetles or cellar beetles.
They are lovers of darkness and are to be found in vaults, cellars, caves and even
coal mines. They have no wings and if disturbed rise up on their long legs, looking
rather like large spiders. They also emit an ill-smelling fluid if molested. The species
shown here, *Blaps gigas,* is one of the largest of them

85

86

85, 86, 87 *Akis italica* (85), like *Blaps,* is one of the
Tenebrionidae, but is elegantly sculptured and quite a handsome
beetle. It lives above the ground in dry, stony places.
Neoclytus acuminatus (86) and *Phytoecia coerulea* (87) are members
of the Cerambycidae or longhorn beetles, whose most outstanding
characteristic is their very long antennae, which sometimes exceed
the whole body in length. Like those of the Buprestidae their larvae
burrow in wood, and sometimes they take years to complete their
development. That of the house longhorn, *Hylotrupes bajulus,*
sometimes damages structural timbers in buildings. Its larva usually
takes from three to six years to develop, but has been known to feed
for thirty-two years, and is thus the longest lived of any known
insect. *Neoclytus acuminatus* is coloured and marked rather like a
wasp, and may derive some protection from its enemies by this
resemblance.

88

89

88–89 Two more longhorn beetles are shown on this page.
Cerambyx cerdo (88) is nearly two inches long with antennae half as
long again. The larvae live in the trunks of oak trees, often doing
considerable damage, and take four years to reach maturity.
Macrodontia cervicornis (89) is a very large South American species
with an overall length of nearly six inches. It lacks the long antennae
of the typical longhorns, but its jaws are almost as overdeveloped as
those of the stag beetle (68). Its pattern of light and dark brown
scroll-like markings provide effective camouflage on the jungle floor,
and it is hard to find in spite of its great size.

90

90 Many readers will recognise at once this photograph of the notorious Colorado potato beetle, *Leptinotarsa decemlineata*. It was discovered in 1823 on an early expedition into the Rocky Mountains, feeding on the buffalo burr. This plant is a member of the nightshade family (Solenaceae) to which the potato also belongs. At first the beetle was comparatively rare and entirely harmless, but when potato culture came to be introduced into the western States the beetle unfortunately found its leaves to be acceptable as food. It reached the Atlantic seaboard of North America in 1874 and appeared in the Bordeaux region of France about 1920. Now the beetle and its gaudy black-and-orange larva are all too familiar in potato fields throughout Europe and in North America from Texas to Canada. Its ability to thrive in a range of climates from subtropical to almost arctic is most unusual among insects.

91

92

91, 92, 93 The minute beetle *Hispa testacea* (91) is covered with spines like a miniature porcupine. Its larvae feed by burrowing between the upper and lower layers of leaves. This mode of feeding, commonly known as 'leaf-mining' is also characteristic of a large number of small moths and of certain flies.

Beetles are the most numerous and diverse of all insects, and as they are to other insects, so are the weevils (Curculionidae) to the rest of the beetles. 40,000 species of weevils have already been described and named and hundreds more are discovered every year.

Their most characteristic feature is a long snout or proboscis, at the end of which are the jaws. Often the antennae arise from a point half way along the snout and can be folded back into a groove on each side of it. Both these features are well seen in *Curculio elephas* (92), which uses its snout to bore into chestnuts and acorns, inside which it lays its eggs. *Cyprus angustus* (93) is also a weevil, but it has the snout much reduced in length.

94 This photograph shows details of the snout of a tropical species of weevil much enlarged. It is unusual in having a coat of silky hairs, but this does not obscure the details of its structure. The jaws can be clearly seen protruding from the tip, and the 'elbowed' antennae are lifted a little way out of the groove into which they can be fitted.

95, 96 Hymenoptera. This important group of insects includes bees, wasps, ants and a number of other less familiar types. Among the best known of them are the social wasps, which make wonderful 'paper' nests from a pulp of chewed-up wood. The nest starts as quite a small structure (95), but when fully populated it contains hundreds of hexagonal cells (96) which accommodate the larvae and pupae.

95

96

97

97–100 Hymenoptera. The sawflies (Tenthredinoidea) can be distinguished from bees and wasps by the absence of a narrow waist between thorax and abdomen. They also have no sting, though the ovipositor or egg-laying organ of the female may look very like one. The species shown (97) has wasp-like markings, but by no means all sawflies are so coloured. Their larvae are 'caterpillars', rather like those of moths, and many of them feed in the same way on the leaves of trees and shrubs. The name 'sawfly' derives from the appearance of the ovipositor of many of them, which is serrated like a saw and used for cutting slits in stems and leaves for insertion of the eggs. The ichneumon wasps all have the habit of laying their eggs in the bodies of other insects (usually of the larva or pupa) or of spiders. When the eggs hatch the larvae live as parasites inside the host, slowly devouring it as it grows and finally killing it when it comes to full size. They destroy enormous numbers of insects, including many that are harmful.

The cuckoo wasps are parasites of a different kind. They lay their eggs in the nests of solitary wasps and bees and their young grow up at the expense of the larvae who are the legitimate nestlings. The parasites may eat the store of food or the larvae themselves. Many cuckoo wasps have brilliant metallic colours, as the two species *Terachrysis semicincta* (99) and *Stilbum cyanurum* (100) well show.

98

99

100

102

103

101, 102, 103 A great number of minute Hymenoptera are responsible for producing on trees and plants the curious growths that we call galls. The eggs are inserted into the stem or leaf and the plant reacts by growing in a peculiar manner and producing a mass of tissue of some particular form which is the same for each species of gall wasp. This mass of tissue or gall affords a food supply for the larvae. Three kinds of gall are shown here, that of *Cynips calicis* (101), shaped like a hood, and the 'marble galls' of *Cynips kollari* (102); both these are formed on oak. The bedeguar gall (103) caused by *Rhodites rosae* is a mass of fibrous tissue, crimson or pink when young, brown in its later stages. It is found on rose bushes.

104

104-105 Ants. *Camponotus ligniperda* (104) is one of the so-called carpenter ants, which burrow in wood to make their nests. They may inhabit dead stumps and logs, in which case they do no harm, or they may bore in living wood and do serious damage. The wood ant, *Formica rufa* (105) makes mounds of dry vegetable debris in woods, which are really the roof or thatch of the underground nest. This ant destroys great numbers of caterpillars and other insects which damage trees, and is regarded with favour on this account by foresters. It is even used in biological control by conveying entire nests to forests where the ant is absent and establishing it in these new localities. The wood ant defends itself by biting and by squirting a jet of formic acid from the hinder end of its body. By adopting the pose shown in the photograph it is able to direct the jet forwards.

107

106

106–110 Hymenoptera. Most of the wasps and bees carry a sting, and some of the species which live in large colonies, the social bees and wasps, are formidable when they fly out in a swarm to attack an intruder. The hornet (106) and the wasp, *Vespula* (110) are among these. The 'portrait' of a wasp (110) shows that these insects are armed with strong jaws as well as stings. Bumblebees, *Bombus* (108) have stings but never attack in great numbers, and the same is true of the large carpenter bees, of which *Xylocopa violacea* (107) is an example. These bees bore holes in wood to make their nests. The solitary wasps of the genus *Pepsis* (109) use their stings to subdue and paralyse large spiders, which they then store in burrows as provender for their larvae.

108

109